BILINGUAL ENGLISH-SPANISH ASSESSMENT™

Inventory to Assess Language Knowledge (ITALK)

NOTE: This form contains both home and school surveys to be completed by SLP professionals during interviews with parent/s and teacher/s.

Name: ______________________ Sex: ❒ M ❒ F Test date: ______ yr ______ mo ______ days

School: ______________________ Grade: ______ Birth date: ______ yr ______ mo ______ days

Examiner: ______________________ Age: ______ yr ______ mo ______ days

Who was interviewed: ❒ **Parent/Guardian** ❒ **Teacher**

ITALK SCORE SUMMARY

ENTER THE HIGHEST AVERAGE AND CIRCLE THE LANGUAGE

SCHOOL FORM: __________ **ENGLISH** **SPANISH**

HOME FORM: __________ **ENGLISH** **SPANISH**

Score Interpretation: **If highest average score ≥4.18, no concerns**
If highest average score <4.18, speech-language assessment is indicated

I0737514

9 781681 252858

ITALK-HOME FORM

We would like you to rate how well your child uses English and Spanish. Rate the child's proficiency in each language using the following scales.

Nos gustaría que usted indique qué bien usa su hijo/a el inglés y/o el español. Use las siguientes escalas para clasificar sus habilidades en los dos idiomas.

VOCABULARY PROFICIENCY / HABILIDAD DEL VOCABULARIO

Vocabulary Proficiency refers to how often the child uses home vocabulary (e.g., food or clothing names) and academic vocabulary (e.g., science terms) in each language.

Circle the appropriate level for each language.

Habilidad del Vocabulario se refiere a la frecuencia con que su hijo/a usa el vocabulario del hogar (p.ej., nombres de comidas o ropa) y el vocabulario académico (p.ej.,términos/palabras de la ciencia) en cada idioma.

Marque el nivel indicado para cada idioma.

How much **English** vocabulary does your child use from the words s/he learns at home (e.g., food, clothing) or school (e.g., science terms)? Del vocabulario que aprende en el hogar (nombres de comidas o ropa) y en la escuela (p.ej., palabras de la ciencia), ¿cuántas palabras usa su hijo/a en **inglés**?		How much **Spanish** vocabulary does your child use from the words s/he learns at home (e.g., food, clothing) or school (e.g., science terms)? Del vocabulario que aprende en el hogar (nombres de comidas o ropa) y en la escuela (p.ej., palabras de la ciencia), ¿cuántas palabras usa su hijo/a en **español**?	
Does not speak in the indicated language./ No habla el idioma indicado.	—	Does not speak in the indicated language./ No habla el idioma indicado.	—
A few words/unas pocas palabras	1	A few words/unas pocas palabras	1
A limited range of words/poca variedad de palabras	2	A limited range of words/poca variedad de palabras	2
Some words/algunas palabras	3	Some words/algunas palabras	3
Many words/muchas palabras	4	Many words/muchas palabras	4
Extensive vocabulary/vocabulario amplio	5	Extensive vocabulary/vocabulario amplio	5
DK—Do not know/No sé	—	DK—Do not know/No sé	—

SPEECH PROFICIENCY / HABILIDAD DEL HABLA

Speech Proficiency refers to how easily the child can be understood in each language.

Circle the indicated level for each language.

Habilidad del Habla se refiere a la facilidad con que los demás entienden a su hijo/a en cada idioma.

Marque el nivel indicado para cada idioma.

How often can you understand your child's speech in **English**? Difficulties in this area might be noted when a child mispronounces a sound such as /r/ or /s/ or a cluster of sounds (e.g., /sk/), or omits part of a word (e.g., says "evator" for "elevator"). ¿Con qué frecuencia puede Ud. entender el habla de su hijo/a en **inglés**? Las dificultades en esta área se notan cuando el niño/a no pronuncia sonidos como /r/ o /s/, un grupo de sonidos (p.ej., /sk/) u omite parte de una palabra (p.ej., dice "evator" en vez de "elevator").		How often can you understand your child's speech in **Spanish**? Difficulties in this area might be noted when a child mispronounces a sound such as /r/ or /s/ or a cluster of sounds (e.g., /st/), or omits part of a word (e.g., says "maposa" for "mariposa"). ¿Con qué frecuencia puede Ud. entender el habla de su hijo/a en **español**? Las dificultades en este área se notan cuando el niño/a no pronuncia sonidos como /r/ o /s/, un grupo de sonidos (p.ej., /st/) u omite parte de una palabra (p.ej., dice "maposa" en vez de "mariposa").	
Does not speak in the indicated language./ No habla el idioma indicado.	—	Does not speak in the indicated language./ No habla el idioma indicado.	—
Never/Nunca	1	Never/Nunca	1
Rarely/Rara la vez	2	Rarely/Rara la vez	2
Sometimes/A veces	3	Sometimes/A veces	3
Very often/Casi siempre	4	Very often/Casi siempre	4
Always/Siempre	5	Always/Siempre	5
DK—Do not know/No sé	—	DK—Do not know/No sé	—

SENTENCE PRODUCTION PROFICIENCY / HABILIDAD DE LA PRODUCCIÓN DE ORACIONES

Sentence Production Proficiency refers to the usual length of the child's sentences when he or she is conversing, responding in class, or telling a story.

Circle the indicated level for each language.

Habilidad de la Producción de Oraciones se refiere a qué tan largas son las oraciones de su hijo/a cuando está charlando, respondiendo en clase, o contando un cuento.

Marque el nivel indicado para cada idioma.

How long are your child's sentences in **English** typically? (Remember that children commonly use sentences of a certain length but when answering a question such as "Would you like a cookie?" may use sentences that are shorter or longer than the usual length.) ¿Qué tan largas son las oraciones de su hijo/a en **inglés** típicamente? (Recuerde que los niños usan oraciones cortas y largas. Usan oraciones cortas cuando están contestando una pregunta por ejemplo, "Would you like a cookie?")		How long are your child's sentences in **Spanish** typically? (Remember that children commonly use sentences of a certain length but when answering a question such as "¿Quieres una galleta?" may use sentences that are shorter or longer than the usual length.) ¿Qué tan largas son las oraciones de su hijo/a en **español** típicamente? (Recuerde que los niños usan oraciones cortas y largas. Usan oraciones cortas cuando están contestando una pregunta por ejemplo, "¿Quieres una galleta?")	
Does not speak in the indicated language./ No habla el idioma indicado.	—	Does not speak in the indicated language./ No habla el idioma indicado.	—
1–2 words/palabras	1	1–2 words/palabras	1
2–3 words/palabras	2	2–3 words/palabras	2
3–4 words/palabras	3	3–4 words/palabras	3
4–5 words/palabras	4	4–5 words/palabras	4
5 or more words/5 o más palabras	5	5 or more words/5 o más palabras	5
DK—Do not know/No sabe	—	DK—Do not know/No sabe	—

GRAMMATICAL PROFICIENCY / HABILIDAD GRAMATICAL

Grammatical Proficiency refers to the grammatical acceptability.

Circle the indicated level for each language.

Habilidad Gramatical se refiere a la frecuencia del uso de oraciones correctas.

Marque el nivel indicado para cada idioma.

How often does your child produce well-formed sentences in **English** when conversing or telling stories? Some forms that may be difficult in English are past-tense forms (e.g., *walked*) or present-tense forms (e.g., *walks*). ¿Con qué frecuencia produce su hijo/a oraciones bien formadas en **inglés** cuando está conversado o contando cuentos? Entre las formas difíciles en inglés son el tiempo pasado (p.ej., *walked*) y el presente (p.ej., *walks*).	
Does not speak in the indicated language./ No habla el idioma indicado.	—
Never/Nunca	1
Rarely/Rara la vez	2
Sometimes/A veces	3
Very often/Casi siempre	4
Always/Siempre	5
DK—Do not know/No sé	—

How often does your child produce well-formed sentences in **Spanish** when conversing or telling stories? In Spanish, children might have trouble with articles (el *naranja* instead of la *naranja*) or pronouns such as lo *comió* (referring to the orange) instead of la *comió*. ¿Con qué frecuencia produce su hijo/a oraciones bien formadas en **español** cuando está conversado o contando cuentos? En español, los niños pueden tener dificultad con los artículos (el *naranja* en vez de la *naranja*) o pronombres (por ejemplo, lo *comió* en vez de la *comió*).	
Does not speak in the indicated language./ No habla el idioma indicado.	—
Never/Nunca	1
Rarely/Rara la vez	2
Sometimes/A veces	3
Very often/Casi siempre	4
Always/Siempre	5
DK—Do not know/No sé	—

COMPREHENSION PROFICIENCY / HABILIDAD DE LA COMPRENSIÓN

Comprehension Proficiency refers to how easily the child understands each language.

Circle the indicated level for each language.

Habilidad de la Comprensión se refiere a la facilidad con que su hijo/a entiende cada idioma.

Marque el nivel indicado para cada idioma.

How often does your child understand what is said in **English**? Difficulties in this area might be noted when s/he frequently asks for repetition or only attends to part of what you say (e.g., last part of a story, one part of a series of instructions). ¿Con qué frecuencia entiende su hijo/a lo que se dice en **inglés**? Por ejemplo, si Ud. nota que pide con frecuencia que Ud. repita o si atiende solamente parte de lo que Ud. dice (p.ej., la parte final de un cuento, parte de una serie de instrucciones).	
Does not understand the indicated language./ No entiende el idioma indicado.	—
Never/Nunca	1
Rarely/Rara la vez	2
Sometimes/A veces	3
Very often/Casi siempre	4
Always/Siempre	5
DK—Do not know/No sé	—

How often does your child understand what is said in **Spanish**? Difficulties in this area might be noted when s/he frequently asks for repetition or only attends to part of what you say (e.g., last part of a story, one part of a series of instructions). ¿Con qué frecuencia entiende su hijo/a lo que se dice en **español**? Por ejemplo, si Ud. nota que pide con frecuencia que Ud. repita o si atiende solamente parte de lo que Ud. dice (p.ej., la parte final de un cuento, parte de una serie de instrucciones).	
Does not understand the indicated language./ No entiende el idioma indicado.	—
Never/Nunca	1
Rarely/Rara la vez	2
Sometimes/A veces	3
Very often/Casi siempre	4
Always/Siempre	5
DK—Do not know/No sé	—

OVERALL LANGUAGE PERFORMANCE

Are you concerned about the way your child talks? ¿Se preocupa por la manera en que habla su hijo/a?

❒ Yes/Sí ❒ No

If yes, please describe your concern. Si se preocupa, explique porque se preocupa.

____

____

____

ITALK-HOME SUMMARY:

Enter and average scores from the ITALK-Home Form.

English	Score	Spanish	Score
Vocabulary		Vocabulary	
Speech		Speech	
Sentence Production		Sentence Production	
Grammar		Grammar	
Comprehension		Comprehension	
TOTAL		**TOTAL**	
Divide total by number of completed indicators **AVERAGE**		Divide total by number of completed indicators **AVERAGE**	

Enter Highest Average Here

[ ]

Scoring Interpretation: **If highest average ≥4.18, no concerns**
If highest average < 4.18, speech-language assessment is indicated

NEXT STEPS: Transfer the highest average scores (Home <u>and</u> School) to the ITALK Score Summary section on the front page of this form <u>and</u> to the section on ITALK on the back page of each Protocol.

ITALK-SCHOOL FORM

Please use the following scales to report language use and proficiency. Some children will achieve the same rating in both languages whereas other children's ratings may vary across languages or across skills/domains.

VOCABULARY PROFICIENCY

Vocabulary Proficiency refers to how well the child uses home vocabulary (e.g., food or clothing names) and academic vocabulary (e.g., color names, science terms) in each language.

Circle the appropriate level for each language.

How much **English** vocabulary does the child use from the words s/he learns at home (e.g., food, clothing) or school (e.g., science terms)?		How much **Spanish** vocabulary does the child use from the words s/he learns at home (e.g., food, clothing) or school (e.g., science terms)?	
Does not speak in the indicated language.	—	Does not speak in the indicated language.	—
A few words	1	A few words	1
A limited range of words	2	A limited range of words	2
Some words	3	Some words	3
Many words	4	Many words	4
Extensive vocabulary	5	Extensive vocabulary	5
DK—Do not know	—	DK—Do not know	—

SPEECH PROFICIENCY

Speech Proficiency refers to how easily the child can be understood in each language.

Circle the appropriate level for each language.

How often can you understand the child's speech in **English**? Difficulties in this area might be noted when a child mispronounces a sound such as /r/ or /s/ or a cluster of sounds (e.g., /sk/), or omits part of a word (e.g., says "evator" for "elevator").		How often can you understand the child's speech in **Spanish**? Difficulties in this area might be noted when a child mispronounces a sound such as /r/ or /s/ or a cluster of sounds (e.g., /st/), or omits part of a word (e.g., says "maposa" for "mariposa").	
Does not speak in the indicated language.	—	Does not speak in the indicated language.	—
Never	1	Never	1
Rarely	2	Rarely	2
Sometimes	3	Sometimes	3
Very often	4	Very often	4
Always	5	Always	5
DK—Do not know	—	DK—Do not know	—

SENTENCE PRODUCTION PROFICIENCY

Sentence Production Proficiency refers to the usual length of the child's sentences when he or she is conversing, responding in class, or telling a story.

Circle the appropriate level for each language.

How long are the child's sentences in **English** typically? (Remember that children commonly use sentences of a certain length but regularly use sentences that are shorter when they are answering a question such as "Would you like a cookie?" or longer than the usual length.)		How long are the child's sentences in **Spanish** typically? (Remember that children commonly use sentences of a certain length but regularly use sentences that are shorter when they are answering a question such as "¿Quieres una galleta?" or longer than the usual length.)	
Does not speak in the indicated language.	—	Does not speak in the indicated language.	—
1–2 words	1	1–2 words	1
2–3 words	2	2–3 words	2
3–4 words	3	3–4 words	3
4–5 words	4	4–5 words	4
5 or more words	5	5 or more words	5
DK—Do not know	—	DK—Do not know	—

GRAMMATICAL PROFICIENCY

Grammatical Proficiency refers to the grammatical acceptability of the child's sentences when he or she is conversing, responding in class, or telling a story.

Circle the appropriate level for each language.

How often does the child produce well-formed sentences in **English** when conversing or telling stories? Some forms that may be difficult in English are past-tense forms (e.g., *he walked*) or present-tense forms (e.g., *he walks*).		How often does the child produce well-formed sentences in **Spanish** when conversing or telling stories? In Spanish, children might have trouble with articles (*el niño comió el naranja* instead of *el niño comió la naranja*) or pronouns/gender such as *lo comió* (referring to the orange) instead of *la comió*.	
Does not speak in the indicated language.	—	Does not speak in the indicated language.	—
Never	1	Never	1
Rarely	2	Rarely	2
Sometimes	3	Sometimes	3
Very often	4	Very often	4
Always	5	Always	5
DK—Do not know	—	DK—Do not know	—

COMPREHENSION PROFICIENCY

Comprehension Proficiency refers to how easily the child understands each language.

Circle the appropriate level for each language.

How often does the child understand what is said in **English**? Difficulties in this area might be noted when s/he frequently asks for repetition or only attends to part of what you say (e.g., last part of a story, one part of a series of instructions).	
Does not speak in the indicated language.	—
Never	1
Rarely	2
Sometimes	3
Very often	4
Always	5
DK—Do not know	—

How often does the child understand what is said in **Spanish**? Difficulties in this area might be noted when s/he frequently asks for repetition or only attends to part of what you say (e.g., last part of a story, one part of a series of instructions).	
Does not speak in the indicated language.	—
Never	1
Rarely	2
Sometimes	3
Very often	4
Always	5
DK—Do not know	—

ITALK CLINICAL SUMMARY

Enter and average scores from the ITALK-School Form.

English	**Score**
Vocabulary	
Speech	
Sentence Production	
Grammar	
Comprehension	
TOTAL	
Divide total by number of completed indicators **AVERAGE**	

Spanish	**Score**
Vocabulary	
Speech	
Sentence Production	
Grammar	
Comprehension	
TOTAL	
Divide total by number of completed indicators **AVERAGE**	

Enter Highest Average Here

Scoring Interpretation: **If highest average score ≥4.18, no concerns**
If highest average score <4.18, speech-language assessment is indicated

NEXT STEPS: Transfer the highest average scores (Home and School) to the ITALK Score Summary section on the front page of this form and to the section on ITALK on the back page of each Protocol.